Kipper ran to get Mum.

1

Floppy ran at the chicken.

The chicken ran at Floppy.

peck
peck
peck

Floppy ran into the shed.

The chicken sat on a box.

It ran at Dad.

Dad shut it in a pen.

Biff put mash in a dish.

8

Biff and Chip fed Jack.

Cock-a-doodle-doo!

Mum and Dad got up.

Biff, Chip and Kipper got up too.